I hate reality but, you know, where else can you get a good steak dinner?

– *Woody Allen*

The Dubliner
100 Best Restaurants

By Domini Kemp and Trevor White

The Dubliner 100 Best Restaurants 2002
by Domini Kemp and Trevor White.
Photography and Design by Joanne Murphy.
Design Consultant Greville Edwards.

First Edition, Published July 2002.
ISBN 0-9542188-0-9

The Dubliner

Published by Dubliner Media Limited
23 Wicklow Street, Dublin 2.
Telephone 353 1 635 9822 *email* dining@thedubliner.ie

Contents

"WHO DRINKS OUR WINES?"

Nathelie Greve, *Sommelier*.
Chapter One Restaurant, Dublin.

Nisea Doddy, *Sommelier*.
Shanahans Restaurant, Dublin.

"WE DO".

For Nisea and Nathelie wine is a way of life.
Fine wines are not only crucial to their professional lives, they are also vital
to any great night out on the town. These women are two of Ireland's
youngest sommeliers and to be at the top of their profession means demanding
the best at all times. The exclusive Torres range of wines from Woodford Bourne
meets their discriminating tastes.
What's your story?

Foreword

The marriage of fine wine and great food is one of the things that truly makes life worth living. Woodford Bourne has provided Irish men and women with the best wines from all over the world for over two hundred years. Indeed, the motto inscribed on our very first warehouse was "Vintage wines aged to perfection for the good people of Ireland."

Many of the establishments reviewed in *The Dubliner 100 Best Restaurants* offer fine wines such as Niebaum Coppola, Bollinger, Brown Brothers and Torres – all are exclusively imported by Woodford Bourne. In sponsoring this book, we're promoting a classic combination – fine wine and great food – just as we have for over two centuries. I hope you enjoy discovering the best restaurants that our city has to offer – and perhaps you might raise the occasional glass!

Ken Peare
Managing Director
Woodford Bourne

Introduction

When foreign journalists come to Dublin, they always have too much to drink. We know this, because their bleary-eyed articles read like the musings of a hungover bride, with a dim recollection of wedding night mischief. That's why critics from normally sober newspapers say such nice things about the food. If you took their rave reviews at face value, you might well believe that we're living through a "culinary revolution" (*New York Times*) or even that the city is a "gourmet paradise" (*Vogue*).

The truth doesn't make for easy headlines. Are there 100 great restaurants in the capital? Probably not. This book always seemed optimistic: the service in most restaurants would embarrass a Prague taxi driver, and many over-charge for food that does *not* deserve an audience. A lot of chefs lack basic skills and, what's worse, they haven't the ambition to go and learn from the French, the Italians – hell, anyone!

However, standards have undoubtedly risen over the last ten years, and there are some outstanding restaurants in Dublin today. They are owned by people for whom a restaurant is more than simply a business. They work with suppliers who insist on quality. Their staff are professionals, and their customers are people who aren't afraid to demand the best.

So read between the lines. You can eat very well in Dublin, and many of the restaurants reviewed in this book will satisfy the most discerning diner. We've probably been a bit too kind in parts, but then, we want to eat lunch in this town again.

Finally, if you don't agree with *our* reviews, why don't you write your own? We print a reader's review in *The Dubliner* each month, and we always love to hear from other diners. It's good to know what chefs get up to when the critics have all gone home.

Domini Kemp and Trevor White
July 2002

A Little Map

First line of Address
Second line of Address
Final line of Address

Telephone Number

HOW TO USE THIS BOOK: Don't go looking for rankings. There aren't any. Rather, this book showcases 100 restaurants in the city and county of Dublin that deserve your business. They are listed in alphabetical order. At the bottom of each entry, a bar across the page lists the postal district, the type of restaurant and the price range. We haven't used scientific criteria to determine the price of an average meal, which is indicated by the sloping bar. As you will see, the vast majority of restaurants are quite expensive or *very* expensive. We have also included a floating section called *Pundit Pie,* a survey of the best Irish restaurant critics; what they like, and who they admire. Finally, there are two indexes at the back of this book.

1 Type of Restaurant

Price

The Dubliner
100
Best Restaurants

101 Talbot

101 Talbot Street
Dublin 1
(*874 5011*

Actors, financiers and weary shoppers are drawn to this
quirky but unpretentious oasis for gourmets on the north
side of the city centre. Consistency and value are the
buzzwords here (but don't go looking for luxury). Starters
include smoked haddock chowder (€6.30), homemade pork,
apricot and sage sausage (€5.00) and pitta with bean, olive
and roast garlic dip (€4.45). Main courses include chargrilled
sirloin steak with green peppercorn sauce (€17.15), roast
vegetable, walnut and goats cheese strudel (€12.60), and
grilled swordfish with smoked garlic and chilli butter
(€17.15). Menu changes weekly and special diets are happily
accommodated; 40% of the menu is vegan friendly.

Modern Irish

Antica Venezia

97 Ashfield Road
Ranelagh
Dublin 6W
497 4112

Tuesday night, 8.00pm – from the outside of this small, intimate corner bistro, it looks as if they're about to call it a day. Step inside: a different story. Capable Antipodean waitress and surly Italian gent cope smooth as butter with the simultaneous invasion of posh locals. There's something good going on in the kitchen – not spectacular, but decent enough. Mushrooms stuffed with ricotta and deep fried mozzarella (€5) were tasty, if under-cooked (a recurring issue), crostini with Parma ham and mozzarella (€5) was delicious. Mains: calzone (€13.90) was full of flavour but needed another few minutes in the oven, and the lamb chops were blue as opposed to pink, with a very tasty mushroom sauce (€16.45). Despite some reservations, this is worth discovering if you live in the area.

Italian 6W

Aqua

1 West Pier
Howth
County Dublin
832 0690

Forgive the new age soundtrack. Located in the former home of Howth Yacht Club, Aqua has a sprawling dining room with fine views, a good atmosphere and some of the best seafood on the northside. Chef Brian Daly's menu changes with the catch; on the day we visited, seared tuna (€27) and whole black sole meuniere (€37) stood out. Both were impressive, simply cooked to allow the fresh fish dominate (you'd know Mr Daly served his apprenticeship under Johnny Cooke). However, the duck confit (€24) was a gloomy reminder that this is a primarily a seafood experience. Decor is modern, with clean lines and a minimalist feel. Alas, many dishes are minimalist too, satisfying the slightest of appetites.

Avoca Café

Suffolk Street
Dublin 2
672 6019

There are just a few good spots for Sunday brunch in Dublin.
This is one of them. *Schlep* up to the top floor of the superb Avoca
store, and join the ranks of posh mummies, country grannies
and local queens who happily queue for a table. Ignore bawling
kids, smile back at the cheerful wait-staff (there's a 10% service
charge) and enjoy a little live jazz – too loud for granny…. beware!
After a shaky start, the food is now consistent. Start with a
selection of Avoca's toasted breads with homemade jams
(€2.50), or try the sweetcorn and coriander chowder with a
tomato salsa (€4.35). Then have the city's best sandwich: open
crab on Avoca's multi-seed bread, with homemade mayo and
sweet cucumber pickle (€10). Wash it down with a glass of *real*
orange juice (€2.50). Yes, this is Avoca-Lite for townies, but so
what? Upbeat, bright and outrageously healthy, it's just like a
trip to the real Avoca – minus Sunday drivers.

Modern Irish 2

Aya

49-52 Clarendon Street
Dublin 2
677 1544

Society queens like Alison O'Reilly love Dublin's only conveyer belt sushi bar, which is prettier than London's chain ones (if just as anodyne). Try exotic delights like nigiri (€4.50) and temaki (€5.40), or stick to Western-influenced fare like deep-fried king prawns (€5.70). The set lunch menu is excellent value at €16.90 for four courses. But if lunch means hassle and the office beckons, order a sushi box on-line. Specials change daily so you can sample the most exciting thing on the menu and still get value for money. And for dinner at home, raid the delicatessen next door for spicy wasabi and jars of pickled ginger. Minor objection: this is sushi for the conservative Irish palate. But whose fault is that?

2 Japanese

Il Baccaro

9 Eustace Street
Temple Bar
Dublin 2
671 4597

This grungy Italian is run by men who growl and women who smile before disappearing to deal with other customers – both are over-worked. Occupying a cosy basement vault across the square from Eden, Il Baccaro couldn't be less like that clinical space. Order plenty of starters, loads of wine (stay well away from the house red) and be very careful about picking main courses. Several are ruined by too much Ragu (and not the sort Mama used to make). All sounds a wee bit grim? Not a bit of it. The atmosphere is electric, and Il Baccaro is quite cheap too – you can stuff yourself and get fairly merry for €25. But remember to stick to the basics. Have bruschetta with olive oil and garlic, bresaola grana e rucola, roast potatoes with garlic and rosemary and a Caprese salad.

Italian 2

Bang

11 Merrion Row
Dublin 2
676 0898

We've known Simon and Christian Stokes for 15 years, and
we still can't tell them apart. Both are young, charming and
extremely handsome. The twins' chic restaurant on Merrion
Row (beside the Unicorn, which is co-owned by their dad,
Jeff) is crammed with gourmet admirers – it's pure co-
incidence that many are female. Most of their staff – like
Kelvin and Aibhinn – are equally beautiful, which is nice if
your guest is a dog. Chef Lorcan Cribbin did a stint in The Ivy
(London, darling) before returning home. We usually start
with the scallops with mousseline potatoes and pancetta
(€11.90) and follow with Thai baked sea bass (€20) served
with fragrant rice and snake beans. Good desserts too: try the
Scandinavian white berries with chocolate sauce (€6.50).
Probably the most fashionable restaurant in the city.

Beaufield Mews

Woodlands Avenue
Stillorgan
County Dublin
288 0375

Not the best restaurant in Dublin – but certainly one of the oldest. Beaufield Mews lies at the end of a secluded avenue in otherwise bland suburbia; now 51 years old, it is surrounded by rose gardens and ancient courtyards. Owner Jill Cox is a passionate antique collector and this is evident throughout. Staff are friendly and efficient, making for a more laid-back experience than the surroundings would suggest. Chef Derval Hooper does a fine roast rack of lamb with mustard and herb crust (€23). Desserts are also good; try the balsamic vinegar ice-cream with rosemary tuiles (€5). Homemade breads, chutneys and relishes are all offered at reasonable prices, and the wine list offers equally good value. This is the sort of place that granny might enjoy.

CD Traditional Irish

Berkeley Room

The Berkeley Court Hotel
Lansdowne Road
Dublin 4
660 1711

There's something unapologetically old-Dublin about this classy steakhouse in the Berkeley Court. They'll hate that word steakhouse, because the menu also includes a superb selection of poultry, fish and seafood. But let's be honest: the Berkeley Room has long been about the discreet passing of brown envelopes (among *customers*, of course) and fine roast ribs of beef. Here the two go hand in hand, like salt and pepper, Torville and Dean, Brennan and McGowan. If steak and scandal fail to whet your appetite, try the Dublin Bay prawns, flamed and served with diced pears, cream and Calvados (€32) and follow it with a whole black sole, with lemon butter sauce (€45). Sunday lunch is particularly good fun; watch political icons do battle with their children, and *nouveau* stars attempt to use a fish knife. All very amusing – but cheap? No way, sweetie.

Traditional Irish 4

Bijou

47 Highfield Road
Rathgar
Dublin 6
496 1518

Good God, Rathgar is getting rather grand these days. Legal
eagles have restored the avenues and squares to their former
glory and the village has responded with chi-chi delis,
boutiques and antique shops. This two-storey restaurant,
facing the church, is a gorgeous *belle époque* bistro with a
modern twist. Elegant dark wood furniture, art deco
paintings, mirrors and beautiful tableware give it that
expensive Deauville look. The lengthy menu is full of bistro
classics – my twice-cooked crispy duck with orange risotto,
kumquat salsa and Cointreau *jus* was a triumph (€ 21) and
the peppered lamb cutlets with black olive and caper
ratatouille (€ 22.79) were also memorable. Prices are high,
despite the quality of cooking, fine service and the schmoozy
ambience. Cosy and sophisticated, Bijou is the perfect refuge
after a long day at the Tribunals.

The Bistro

4/5 Castle Market
Dublin 2
671 5430

The Bistro has a splendid location, especially on sunny days, when the patio tables are hijacked by professional people watchers (this particular block attracts a huge number of those). Right next door to the ex-home of Cooke's Café, the Bistro is truly a poor relation – much cheaper, rougher and not as formal, but still quite nice all the same. Beware of the service; often excellent, occasionally wretched. And you won't be allowed to nab those outside tables unless you have a full meal. The menu changes regularly. Food is erratic: at the moment, pastas are good, not outstanding. The fish and chips are fine. Bravo for serving sardines! Why do we never see these tasty lads on Irish menus? PS: About that service. On the night before we printed this book, a gang of us had dinner outside the Bistro. We didn't reserve, the party kept growing, we got very drunk. Yet the cheerful young waitress who served us did not frown once.

Blueberry's

15 Main Street
Blackrock
County Dublin
278 8900

After a stint as a sommelier in Guilbaud's, Michel
Deregnieaux took over Blueberry's last September. A few
tweaks to interiors and ambience mean that it's now more
bistro than restaurant. Food is competent: confit tuna
nicoise (€7.75), crostini with goat cheese and Parma ham
(€7.25), French onion soup (€5.50), beef Dianne (sic)
(€20.95). A glass of wine is included with the excellent value
two-course lunch at €14.60 – and it's not plonk. A wine club
on the first Monday of the month sounds like a good idea – a
cheap and cheerful tasting menu is accompanied by selected
wines. Monsieur's enthusiasm and passion make it easy to
forgive occasional kitchen cock-ups.

 French

Bon Appetit

9 St. James Terrace
Malahide
County Dublin
☏ *845 0314*

If fine claret is your thing and you like things classical rather than contemporary, this comfortable old restaurant is a good reason to go Northside. Michael Douglas, Alex Ferguson and CJ Haughey have worshipped at the temple of Monaghan man Patsy McGuirk. Why? "Modern" Irish fare. Stick to fishy classics like Carlingford oysters, Dublin Bay prawns, monkfish with prawns, roast turbot and grilled Dover sole on the bone. Meat and game also put in an appearance; roast crispy duckling, fillet steak. Prices are reasonable, given the rich ambience: about €10 for starters, €25 for mains. An extensive wine list and superb service are the real reasons for making this pilgrimage – unless, of course, you live locally, in which case Patsy is a hero of sorts, and a "genuine" culinary giant.

Traditional Irish CD

Bond

5 Beresford Place
Dublin 1
855 9244

The broker's roar is more subdued than it was last year, but there's still a decent buzz at Bond (the name owes more to finance than espionage). Executives from the IFSC swap gossip at lunchtime, while the odd bemused back-packer, lured by its proximity to Busarus, looks on. The restaurant is informal and stylish, with chunky wooden tables and blue plastic chairs (much nicer than the description suggests). Dinner highlights include the salt and pepper seafood platter (€7.95), and a rack of veal with baby potatoes, shallots and ginger (€27.95). You can buy eight different types of water, but the wine cellar is the real attraction – sommelier Julien le Gentil takes it all very seriously, and the mark-up (retail plus €6.35) is reasonable. Lunchtime regulars used to gourmet sandwich fare will be sorry to learn that the menu has now been revamped as a kind of mini-dinner. But they will return nonetheless; Bond is worth the trek.

Modern Irish

Browne's

22 St. Stephens Green
Dublin 2
638 3939

Quite apart from anything else, you've got to admire Barry
Canny's chutzpah. He ran a very successful place in Glasthule
before opening this townhouse hotel and restaurant right
next door to the Shelbourne (this is a bit like busking outside
a U2 gig). Twelve very comfortable bedrooms include a suite
with a foldaway bed that once belonged to Marilyn Monroe.
Downstairs, there's a handsome 80-seat brasserie, where chef
Sebastian Scheer uses prime Irish ingredients to produce
award winning fare for well-heeled tourists and locals alike.
All very starry, too: John Hurt is a regular, while Michael
Caine and Paul McCartney have both used Browne's as a base
in Dublin. Culinary highlights include a roast duck breast
with coconut flavoured dauphinoise, lime pickled endives
and green chilli and tomato coulis (€22.95). Incidentally,
Browne's do a fine brunch on Sunday – it's child-friendly too.

Bruno's

21 Kildare Street
Dublin 2
(*662 4724*

Never mind the basement setting: Bruno's is worth discovering. Good strong flavours and classic, well-judged cooking from head chef Garrett Byrne. No false niceties or insincere gestures. Starters like confit of rabbit, foie gras with black pudding and ravioli of salmon (all up to €12) display broad French and Italian influences. Clientele? Plenty of regulars, a few chefs and some well-behaved suits. Stand-out dishes include roast sea bream with red pepper tapenade and basil mash (€21.95), and magret of duck with pea purée and sage and potato croquette (€22.95). Finish up with hot rum and raisin pudding, chocolate strudel or lime parfait with strawberry consommé (€6.95). Mediocre wine list. Terms and conditions apply: above comments non-transferable to Temple Bar outlet, which is not in the same league food-wise.

C-Bar

Epicurean Food Hall
Liffey Street
Dublin 1
865 6663

C-Bar used to be a cheap seafood restaurant for the Caviston clan – and quite nice it was too – until they abandoned the city for the safe confines of Glasthule. Derry Clarke of L'Ecrivain took over, and he has now stashed chef Tom Coffey in the kitchen. Never mind the cramped conditions, nor the rash of *Independent* hacks (it's around the corner from Media-Central): this gourmet quick-stop is possibly the best value city centre restaurant. Great fish and chips, seafood cakes, daily specials – try the soft-shell crab risotto – and soup. Plenty of wines by the glass, but no desserts; the idea is that you can run in and have a genuinely delicious meal for about €17. They also sell prepped fish (already filleted, boned and ready to be cooked). Tops off!

Café Bar Deli

South Great Georges Street
Dublin 2
677 1646

It's had a make-over, but you can still feel the ghostly presence of Bewleys in the latest addition to the Bourke-Foyle empire. Right beside the heart of that empire (the Globe) this cheap, no-reservations trattoria looks like yet another winner for those bright young entrepreneurs. Grab a banquette – not the world's most comfortable – and talk Camus over good pizza (average €10), reasonable pasta (€10) and a few hearty salads (from €4.50). The menu is short, unambitious – starters are often better than mains. Try the buffalo mozzarella, avoid the bresaola. Drink real beer on tap (a luxury in Dublin restaurants). Big, bustling, cheap and friendly, customer turnover is high but staff refrain from greedily eyeballing your table. Last time we ate here, main courses were uniformly dull, but six chocolate brownies for dessert were too much even for eight of us.

La Cave

28 South Anne Street
Dublin 2
679 4409

While the pub is the epicentre of Dublin social life, alternatives are useful when your mood doesn't scream for a dirty big pint. La Cave is among the best of these. With its moody lighting, fading lustre and more than a hint of intrigue, it feels like a chic ex-pat hangout in colonial Africa. There's a long wine-list, from affordable house wines by the glass or bottle (around €15) to triple figure clarets. Reasonable Gallic cuisine: either a four-course table d'hote (€27.90) or à la carte, as well as late-night snacks. Try the baked goat's cheese salad (€6). Follow it with the mushroom ravioli, truffle oil and parmesan shavings (€13.90) – but do ask for extra truffle oil! – or the chicken couscous (€15.15). La Cave is a smart venue for first dates – the lighting is kind – and a quiet tipple here is a fine way to end the evening when you're not quite drunk enough for Joy's.

French 2

Cavistons

59 Glasthule Road
Sandycove
County Dublin
280 9120

"Whatever comes in on the day, we sell on the day," says Peter Caviston, who still refuses to open this tiny (26 seats!) seafood restaurant for dinner. There is clearly a strong culinary gene in the Caviston clan. The fish and gourmet food shop next door – now 50 years in the family – is busier than ever, and this six-year old neighbour is fast becoming a Bel-Eire classic. There are not two but *three* sittings for lunch, Tuesday to Saturday, at 12, 1.30 and 3pm; how irritating is that? And don't bother turning up without a reservation – you won't get in. Smart locals like Maeve Binchy, Ali Hewson and Tim Pat Coogan wait until 3pm, by which time the corporates have left and there's no fear of table-thievery. Start with the chowder, or the whole prawns *á la plancha*. Follow with half a lobster or black sole on the bone. What's your secret, Peter? "Let the fish do the talking." What more can we say? Go, eat, worship.

CD Seafood

The Cellar Bar

Merrion Hotel
Merrion Street
Dublin 2
(*603 0600*

So many readers of *The Dubliner* rave about Sunday brunch
here (€8.25-€25) that we expected the space to be jammers
and smoky. Not a bit of it. The experience was pure Merrion –
classy and courteous. First bonus: we were able to book a
table. Second bonus: music was kindly provided by someone
singing something inoffensive. Fantastic eggs Benedict, the
best skinny chips we've had in a while, decent Bloody Marys
and attentive waiters who cheerfully deal with hungover
diners ("Ketchup? No problem, sir."). People watching too;
last time we spotted famous lovers – illicit lovers – who
should *really* have stayed in bed for breakfast. There is also a
sort of afternoon tea buffet with cakes and goodies for
pudding. All very posh: your folks will be impressed.

Modern Irish 2

Chapter One

18/19 Parnell Square
Dublin 1
☎ 873 2266

Yes, the location is hardly handy, and it's in a basement, but
you'll still need to book early to avoid disappointment: Chapter
One offers the best value in town for *haute cuisine*. Since the day it
opened in 1992, chef Ross Lewis and partner Martin Corbett
have poured effort, skill and showmanship into the food rather
than flashy PR stunts. That's why their restaurant is so popular
among other chefs – indeed, many people who work in the
business say Chapter One is where they like to let their hair
down. Try the hake fillet with ratatouille, sautéed potato,
spinach and shellfish sauce (€25.50), or the roast barbary duck,
foie gras farce, glazed parsnip and apple *jus* (€24.75). By the way,
the special pre-theatre dinner (€27.50) is convenient for the Gate
next door; follow Michael Colgan's lead – not advice we'd
normally offer – by coming back for dessert *after* the show.

Modern Irish 1

The Chili Club

1 Anne's Lane
Dublin 2
677 3721

Hidden down a little laneway off South Anne Street, behind a forbidding front door, this tiny Thai restaurant is not spectacular, but has long had a loyal following among local businessmen, savvy shoppers and smart country folk (it's beside the snooty RIAC). Lunch is particularly good value, the service is invariably attentive and the cooking is solid. Our favourite dishes include the Chili Club Selection and the Gaeng Kari Gai, a yellow curry chicken with coconut milk.

PUNDIT PIE *My favourite chefs are sisters Niamh Boylan and Orla Roche, who used to run Roche's Bistro in Malahide. The quality of the seafood in the new Teppanyaki part of Wongs in Castleknock is in a class of its own. Café Blue in Howth does a good value lunch. I predict a revival of unfussy, back to basics, organic food with a particular emphasis on what's in season. The level of service in Irish restaurants is deplorable. Only 1% are up to scratch –* **Ross Golden Bannon** *of the Sunday Business Post.*

China-Sichuan

4 Lower Kilmacud Road
Stillorgan
County Dublin
(288 4817

The location (a row of shops in the "heart" of Stillorgan) and
the interior (formal, or merely dour) leave something to be
desired, but one cannot fault the cooking. Officially
approved by the Chinese government, the China-Sichuan is
arguably the most authentic ethnic restaurant in the city.
David and Julie Hui have bravely resisted the urge to
westernise dishes to curry (sorry) favour with local diners.
However, they will, if pushed, make steak and chips for the
true ignoramus. Gourmets stick to delights like pork shreds
in garlic sauce (€12.70), the smoked duck with pancakes
(€20.32) or black sole with yellow bean sauce (€20.95). One
of us thinks it's the best Chinese in Ireland – the other one
says that honour belongs to a Belfast restaurant.

The Commons

Newman House
85/86 St. Stephen's Green
Dublin 2
478 0530

Michael Fitzgerald's restaurant in the basement of beautiful Newman house is among the top five in the city, and a perennial favourite among tycoons like Michael Smurfit and visiting dignitaries – it is next door to the Department of Foreign Affairs. There's a zen-like calm about the place, the service is usually faultless and you'd better bring several credit cards. Despite a bewildering array of head chefs over the last few years (many have gone on to launch their own places) the modern French cuisine remains remarkably consistent, and current head chef Aidan Byrne has won major plaudits, including a coveted Michelin star. His signature dishes include foie gras with pineapple sorbet, and an assiette of Pyrenees milk-fed lamb with sweet garlic purée.

Cruzzo

Marina Village
Malahide
County Dublin
℡ *845 0599*

Anyone with the audacity to describe their business as "Europe's most spectacular bar and restaurant" has got to be admired for their *chutzpah*, if nothing else. While this plush complex in Malahide's marina falls a little short of the expectations conjured up by that grand claim, it is certainly one of the more innovative new restaurants north of Dublin's city centre. The food is "creative," the staff are attentive, and the ambiance is warm and comfortable. Tuesday nights are particularly good fun, with local hero Des Smith belting out the Sinatra tunes.

PUNDIT PIE *For a quick, cheap lunch I like the noodles at Tribeca. I love the Tea Room and Guilbaud's. Thornton's is the place to go if you're a real foodie and particularly if you have a passion for truffles. L'Ecrivain is the most romantic restaurant in the city, and I also love Dobbins. John O'Byrne is a wonderful host —* **Petra Carter**, *Irish Tatler Magazine.*

Modern European CD

Da Roberto

George's Lane
Blackrock
County Dublin
278 0759

One of the best finds this year, slap bang in the heart of Blackrock. Handsome Italian waiters clad in Armani jeans talk you through a long menu incorporating all those bastardised Italian dishes (think spag-bol) – but here, at least, they are damn tasty. Bona fide buffalo mozzarella, marinated in unctuous olive oil, tonnes of soft, young rocket, lashings of Parma ham, then big bowls of spaghetti carbonara, or ravioli with mushrooms all went down a treat. Really buzzy and casual, with tables adequately spaced, this is a fun, medium priced, cheerful suburban trattoria. Worth a detour.

PUNDIT PIE *My favourite chef is Derry Clarke of L'Ecrivain. He's really passionate about what he does. Citrus is the best new restaurant to have opened in the last year. The most romantic restaurant is the Unicorn in the early evening, and Thornton's if peace counts for the whole evening. The Chili Club is good if you want to sit close to the object of your affections and the Trocadero »*

 Italian

Dali's

63/65 Main Street
Blackrock
County Dublin
☏ *278 0660*

Pretty paintings by the proprietor's wife, soft lighting and excellent front of house staff lend this suburban spot a sophisticated yet homely feel – bit like a posh family dining room. It's probably too fancy to just grab a quick bite in, and prices are quite high. They do a roaring trade, especially on a Friday, when liquid-lunchers sometimes end up staying for dinner (in other words, darling, you may have found your spiritual home). Starters are small and tasty (€5-€11), some of the main courses are huge (€18-€25).

is the place to go after a really good show. The best cheap restaurant in town is the Avoca café, and the most under-rated restaurant is Chapter One. There are too many "fashionable" places offering poor food and putting far too much emphasis on style over substance, and charging too much for it — **Biddy White Lennon**, *President of the Food Writer's Guild.*

Modern Irish CD

Diep Le Shaker

55 Pembroke Lane
Dublin 2
661 1829

Opinions are sharply divided on this bustling Thai restaurant in the heart of media land. Young hotshots like Gerry Purcell are regulars, while older, wiser folk have reservations. Proprietor Matthew Farrell looks and sounds like an English gent, but we know the *real* Mr Farrell. Helen Lucy Burke says Diep serves "emasculated Thai and Chinese food. And who likes a eunuch?" Still, the interior is bright, the tableware is smart and Alan Horca from the Philippines is one of the most courteous waiters in the city. Best dishes include Tom Yum Kai, a spicy chicken soup with lemongrass and chopped coriander, and Sia Rong Hai, a chargrilled sirloin of beef, served with fish sauce, chilli and lime dressing. Fine Thai chicken salad – but what the hell were the strawberries doing in there? God loves a relevant garnish.

2 Thai

Dish

146 Upper Leeson Street
Dublin 4
671 1248

Trevor Browne spent a fortune doing up the old Señor Sassi's
premises, beside Leeson Street bridge. It now feels chic,
modern, elegant – in short, a fine backdrop to Ger Foote's
celebrated cooking. Celebrated? Sycophantic hacks wrote
epic paeans of praise when Dish was in Temple Bar. So what's
this high-profile refugee from our 'cultural' quarter like
today? The menu is well balanced, the service is usually good
– unobtrusive, efficient – and although it has yet to dazzle,
the food certainly shows promise. Best starters are the
shredded confit of duck with a watercress salad and the
grilled scallops with mousseline potato and garlic butter. To
follow, have the pan-fried calves liver. Parents grumble about
'youthful atmosphere.' Ignore: it will do them good.

Dobbins

15 Stephens Lane
Dublin 2
661 3321

Never mind the sawdust, book yourself a booth. Veteran restaurateur John O'Byrne has created a perfect blueprint for the Irish bistro (yes, a very confusing notion). A fine judge of claret, O'Byrne is a jovial host, and regulars swear by this Dublin classic (others just swear at the prices). Nestled among a row of mews houses off Mount Street, Dobbins is usually packed with local suits. Ancient favourites like Dublin Bay prawns, trio of salmon and a fine fillet of Beef also appeal to political animals and rich Americans – but don't expect culinary fireworks.

PUNDIT PIE *Homely food in pleasant places, even if it's all a little "me too." Don't expect too much variety; rather, a decent meal conducive to a good night out. Try Dobbins or L'Ecrivain, but if the wallet extends itself, don't miss Guilbauds. And enjoy it. Our restaurants, like the city itself, provide a welcome and an opportunity to chat. Clearly a hallmark of good dining and frankly, no better place to find it – Ad-man* **Stuart Fogarty** *reviews restaurants for the Irish Marketing Journal.*

Traditional Irish 2

Dunne and Crescenzi

14 South Frederick Street
Dublin 2
677 3815

A little gem owned by Eileen Dunne and Stefano Crescenzi: no more, really, than a handful of tables in an intimate setting that stays open until nine or ten at night. They serve and sell excellent Italian wine, antipasti (€5.70), crostini (€4.50) and panini (Parma ham and mozzarella, €4, roast ham, Tuscan sheep cheese and rocket, €5.10). Lunch on the tiny terrace is fun on a sunny day, and this place is also perfect for pre-dinner drinks. Stefano, together with David Izzo, branched out to open La Corte in the Epicurean Food Hall, where food is equally good and you will get the finest Italian coffee in Dublin. This savvy duo also run Bar Italia on the quays, doing good value breakfasts and lunches. Good operators and genuine hospitality: Izzo may well emerge as an Irish-Italian Terence Conran, with another branch in the IFSC and plans to open in Powerscourt.

L'Ecrivain

109a Lower Baggot Street
Dublin 2
(*661 1919*

This is a fine dining restaurant that encourages *craic* and pleases punters who like a drink but cannot stand the sniffy ambience of Guilbaud's. Head chef Derry Clarke is an old school gent, and his wife, Sally Anne, is a formidable partner. They ushered in the 21st century by re-opening L'Ecrivain after a monster twelve month overhaul. The once-twee interior now feels strikingly modern. Clarke's modern French/Irish cuisine deserves a Michelin star – try the Dublin Bay prawns in ketaifi pastry, or the baked rock oysters in Guinness sabayon. His team cement the claim: Martina Delaney is Dublin's most accommodating sommelier and genial Scotsman Kevin Watson returned to Dublin via London's Lindsay House to become manager here at one of the city's top three restaurants.

Formal 2

Eden

Meeting House Square
Temple Bar
Dublin 2
670 5372

There's an incredibly boring game that Dubliners play, called "What's your favourite restaurant?" It's boring because the answer is so predictable. Rich people say Restaurant Patrick Guilbaud. Gourmet-snobs say Thorntons. And the wise say L'Ecrivain or Chapter One. Eden used to figure somewhere too; indeed, it was once the hottest restaurant in a city that has seen dozens of one-month wonders. Fashion is cruel: the cool blue interior – often compared to a swimming pool – has enduring appeal, and Eleanor Walsh's modern Irish cooking is still a winner. Try the organic lamb's liver and kidneys or the smokies-to-die-for. Unusually for a restaurant in Temple Bar, the waiting staff are cheerful and efficient. Many of them – like manager Orla Murphy – have been here since the day it opened, which must be a good sign. And, on a fine afternoon, Sunday brunch more than justifies the trek into town.

2 Modern Irish

Elephant and Castle

18 Temple Bar
Dublin 2
(679 3121

Kitchen sink drama: Trevor Browne used to work here; he filched their famous recipe for chicken wings. Today, Browne's Tribeca is difficult to get into – reservations are only accepted on the day in question – and the Elephant and Castle is a bit more subdued than it used to be. Don't get the wrong idea: you'll still be asked to bugger off for an hour or so, and E&C is still a firm favourite with locals and visitors alike. But for the first time in nearly ten years, it feels a little weary. Maybe it's because the portions aren't quite as gargantuan as they used to be, and the toilets were a little shabby on our last visit – or is it because Tribeca has stolen its thunder? Either way, the cheeseburger, omelettes and fishcakes are all still worth the wait.

Ely

22 Ely Place
Dublin 2
676 8986

This is the kind of place we'd like to see more of: a cosy, sophisticated wine bar without any sleazy, City of London connotations. Housed in the basement of number 22, where the legendary Shaft nightclub used to be, it is cheery and spacious, with a couple of semi-private nooks and crannies. Staff are informed, hip, fun. Food is an unpretentious jumble of dishes – think oysters (€10.09 for six), bangers and mash (€12.63), fish cakes (€12.63), cheese plate (€10.09). Most of it is very tasty. We love the organic hamburger, but do insist on mash instead of potato salad. Wine, the main business of the place, is available in generous measures by the glass; choose from an extensive list. Perfect for those nights when you really don't fancy more than a glass or two.

Ernie's

Mulberry Gardens
Dublin 4
269 3300

It's hard to say exactly why Ernie's remains so popular after all these years. It's not that the cooking is particularly ambitious; more, perhaps, that Ernie's is a complete experience. For a start, Robert Cahill is the best Maitre d' in Ireland; amusing, savvy and incredibly courteous. Tucked away behind Donnybrook village, Ernie's has always had a wonderful ambience: the interior is well-lit and there's a fine collection of modern Irish art on the walls. To start, try the tian of crabmeat with orange and fennel (€11.50) – generous, fresh and pleasant. The rack of lamb (€25.95) is really good; classic Ernie's fare, with a black olive and tomato sauce. Delicious side orders of vegetables; cooked with care, rather than created as an all-too-obvious afterthought. In short, there's nothing particularly modish about Ernie's, but that's not the point. If you're a fan of, say, Locks, then you'll like this aging gem.

The Exchange

Westin Hotel
College Green
Dublin 2
645 1000

The service is splendid, the view is unusual – right onto
Westmoreland Street – and the interior is light and airy, but
don't expect to meet Major McDowell in this smart hotel
restaurant. It's where senior *Irish Times* management plot
their next move in a battle that is far from over. See them
huddled over poached smoked haddock, served – by an
excellent waiting team – with a rocket and calamari salad
(€12.50). If you're going for the table d'hote menu, try the
Jerusalem artichoke soup with smoked foie gras shavings and
follow it with cumin spiced pan seared tuna. Watch sozzled
hacks toast – with a sigh! – the end of these long lunches.
How entirely appropriate that the Westin Hotel should
provide such ample refuge; a winning blend of youth and age,
it seems like a bastion of civilised values, and yet it's only one
year old! Out with the old etc...

Modern European 2

Fadó

The Mansion House
Dawson Street
Dublin 2
676 7200

The Mansion House has come alive recently; the outgoing
Lord Mayor, Michael Mulcahy, used it to host all manner of
ligs, including parties for dear old dad – *Phoenix* publisher
John – and even for his little brother's wedding reception.
Mere mortals can also sample the good life, in this vast room
next door to the Mansion House. Fadó is one of those
restaurants that simply couldn't have existed ten years ago.
In its confident, self-conscious Irishness it epitomises new
Dublin – in a setting that smacks of heritage. Food also owes
much to tradition, without depending too heavily on bacon
and cabbage type staples. Service is fine and the set lunch
offers good value. Boozy lunches on the terrace are a
splendid way to pass sunny afternoons, but do book ahead,
as you won't be the only one bunking off work. Quibble:
when it's quiet, Fadó can feel like an airplane hangar.

2 Modern Irish

Fitzers

51 Dawson Street
Dublin 2
670 6577

I look at the customers and recognise them from my last visit
here; that was two years ago, pre-make-over, so their loyalty
impresses me. Maybe it's genres I'm recognising, rather than the
faces: trendy business types, young-ladies-who-lunch and smart
mother-daughter combos. It's now a large, airy room – quite
noisy, table and chairs arranged in higgledy-piggledy fashion.
Twice my chair was bumped by a waiter trying to squeeze
through the minute gap between our table and the next. And he
wasn't fat. Fancy salads, pasta, fish and meat are all served in true
Fitzers fashion: large white plates, food stacked in the very centre
and surrounded by a circle of something drizzled. Combinations
such as prawn salad with sweet chilli dip and coriander (€16.45),
pan-fried sea trout with rocket, parmesan and oven dried tomato
(€15.85) or roast breast of chicken with pumpkin seed risotto
cake (€15.90) no longer stun but are, at least, palatable.

Forty Foot

The Pavilion
Dun Laoghaire
County Dublin
284 2982

An ex-bank official called Hugh O'Regan launched many of Dublin's coolest bars. He's now selling them, and concentrating on hotels and restaurants instead. This newcomer sits atop his drop-dead gorgeous bar of the same name (you feel like an extra in a shoot for *Wallpaper* magazine) and both command magnificent views of Dublin Bay. You pay a hefty premium for those views, so insist on a window table. We love the name – a Dublin staple, re-invented – and the logo is fun, too. We had Sunday lunch, served by attentive, courteous staff. The cocktails were good, the food is fine. I had the prawn Thai broth (€9.50) to start, and followed it with medallions of beef, mushrooms, green beans, shallots and red wine sauce (€23.50). The linguini with seafood and fresh herbs (€18.50) was mean on seafood and too loyal, perhaps, to an ancient recipe. It needs a Forty Foot makeover. But there is real talent at work here.

World CD

Les Fréres Jacques

74 Dame Street
Dublin 2
(679 4555

This family-run restaurant on the southern edge of Temple Bar – yes, parking is a nightmare – offers traditional French cuisine. 'Old Parisian' decor – dark greens and creams – is matched by snooty/French service in a space that could do with a revamp. Prices aren't cheap, but for special occasions Les Fréres Jacques is a good bet – particularly at the weekends, when there's a resident pianist. Seafood is the speciality, and they're smart enough to stick to a simple formula: just produce some spanking fresh fish, pan-fry and serve with a few simple accompaniments. Try the grilled black sole with lemon and parsley butter (€35.50). Match-winning desserts include a thin apple tart with rum raisin ice cream (€8.85). Plus: this is one of the few restaurants in the city that offers a decent cheese plate (€10.15).

2   Formal

Fox's Seafood Kitchen

Glencullen
County Dublin
295 5647

If you're looking after uncle Bob from Florida (and you don't feel like fleecing him at Guilbaud's) this is the place to take him. Amazing, isn't it? Tourists have absolutely no interest in our trendy brasseries and new Irish nonsense. They want *Quiet Man* fare – big black pints of Guinness and Irish coffees after a monster feed of oysters, prawn cocktail and seafood plates. And why not? It's not the highest pub in Ireland (The Blue Light, for different reasons) and it's cheesier than a Galtee single, but Fox's is fun. On that basis alone we urge you to throw off the shackles of good taste and buy Oirish, dammit.

Gotham

8 South Anne Street
Dublin 2
(679 5266

Once upon a time the Coffee Inn was every artist's favourite
hangout – grunge-chic way before grunge became chic. In its
place, South Anne Street now boasts the wretched Eddie
Rockets, and the street feels far more clinical. Gotham Café
is no good for ten-spots and illicit encounters with young
French students, 'though it does feel vaguely bohemian
(those *Rolling Stone* covers lend instant cred) and the food is
ten times better than anything the Coffee Inn could muster.
Stick to the pizzas – Chinatown (€11.30) and Tribeca are
our favourites – and avoid the Caesar salad. Jovial singer-
songwriter Leslie Keye waits tables and, while you can't book
a table, staff will happily fetch you from Kehoe's pub when
your table is ready – real Irish service.

Italian 2

Govinda's

4 Aungier Street
Dublin 2
475 0309

With branches in Los Angeles, Paris and Rome, you might assume that Govinda's is one of those super-chic bistros so beloved of celebrities. As it happens, Sinead O'Connor is a regular at this simple, clean vegetarian café. The catch? Govinda's is owned and managed by the Hare Krishnas, who ensure that all dishes are free of caffeine (makes you hyper), garlic (makes you passionate) and mushrooms (makes you ignorant, apparently). In fairness, the Harries are a lot less scary than the Scientologists – the manageress, Nicola, is charming – and Govinda's is a great place for cheap, tasty lunch in town. However, you may have a hard time convincing your mother to darken its doors. Try the moussaka and the cheesy curd paneer with a buttered chapati. Down it with a mango smoothie. Total price? €7.20. *Haribol!*

Gruel

68A Dame Street
Dublin 2
670 7119

You won't be able to reserve a table, it shuts at 9pm and the staff are downright laconic, but this diner has an awful lot going for it. Ben and Mark of the Mermaid Café set it up in response to requests for somewhere with slow food quality and fast food prices. There's a simple, slightly retro feel to Gruel, and nice little touches – like a gallery wall for local artists – but in truth you won't be dazzled by the atmosphere. The food is superb: soup specials (€5.70) change each day – there are fine pizzas (€3.20) too. But the real treat here is the hot roast-in-a-roll sandwich (€5.75): try the roast beef and sundried tomato pesto (Monday) and the roast lamb with apricot chutney (Friday). They also serve a hearty tagine, and *real* freshly squeezed orange juice (€2.50). A fine brunch at the weekends, too. Definitely worth a visit.

The Greenhouse

Harbourmaster Pub
Custom House Docks
Dublin 1
(670 1688

This is where the IFSC meets Canary Wharf. A bright, sophisticated restaurant, the Greenhouse is dwarfed by bold new emblems of high finance, and yet it's just a stone's throw from Sheriff Street. Another outpost in Hugh O'Regan's empire, it's only open for lunch (Monday-Friday, 12-3pm), and it is certainly not cheap (€28 for two courses) but if you're meeting Mr Gekko (or Dermot Desmond), the ambience and the wine list both scream *Deal Clincher*. Service is superb – not too fussy, not too casual – but we've heard that it can be slow sometimes. Head chef Kristan Burness, a Geordie, is a perfectionist, and the food (at least, on the two occasions we have dined here) is consistently good. Highlights include a blue cheese soufflé with a walnut and baby spinach salad, and maize-fed chicken breast with wild mushroom risotto, peas and bacon.

1 Modern Irish

Halo

The Morrison Hotel
Ormond Quay
Dublin 1
878 2421

Anything this trendy is guaranteed to suffer an onslaught from the fashion pack, before suddenly being dumped. Then, after a decent interval, people will start to quietly trickle back. Today, Halo is a good place to bring visitors who think that our capital is a wee bit parochial. However, the high ceilings make some people feel uncomfortable, and its immediate future is uncertain, as the Morrison Hotel is up for sale. In the meantime, Jean Michel Poulot (a Peacock Alley graduate) prepares something called "French-Irish fusion cuisine," which is far tastier than it sounds. Portions are small, leaving plenty of room for dessert. Have the scallops or the John Dory. Try to snag table sixteen. Regulars include Ronan Keating and Shane McGowan, a "true gentleman" according to a friend who works here.

1 French

The Imperial

12a Wicklow Street
Dublin 2
677 2580

When Helen Lucy Burke came back raving about this Chinese
restaurant beside *The Dubliner*, we simply had to try it. We
usually fear the term "spring roll," but the Imperial's "special
spring rolls" (€4.44) were delicious, non-greasy morsels. The
squid cakes (€4.44) had us grasping for more ... and more,
and oh God! We pigged it on the pork and prawn dumplings
(€4.44) as well. You'll also get lobster – real lobster, not the
rubber lump kind – here, and it's cooked the Chinese way:
steady the creature on the chopping block, hack it to
wriggling pieces with a cleaver, then straight into a wok with
peanut-oil, ginger, scallions and some garlic for a flash-fry
(€27.93). We also tried the steamed sea bass (€22.86), soy
sauce chicken (€13.97), roasted duck (€16.51), and a
heavenly thing called choi sum (€13.97) with garlic sauce. No
wonder the Chinese love this place; it is the *real deal*.

Chinese 2

Jacob's Ladder

4 Nassau Street
Dublin 2
670 3865

We've never had dinner at Jacob's Ladder, but have lunch here quite often. It's the discretion we like; in the service, the numbers and the clientele. The dining room is rarely packed. The diners are older, polished, and they always seem to be exchanging top secret information in this small room overlooking Trinity College. Food combines classical French – roast pheasant, parfait of guinea fowl, quails' eggs – with classical Irish – colcannon, champ – and exotic treats like shitake mushrooms. It's usually well presented and plentiful; it would want to be. At €4.85 a starter, €9.95 a main course and €4.50 for pudding with no set menu, this is a pricey lunch. In fact it's just short of Guilbaud's €25 two course table d'hote and the food is hardly comparable. Yet we keep going back. It's a respite in the middle of the working day; restful, luxurious and polite. Take a trusted ally and conspire to rule the world.

2 Modern European

Jaipur

21 Castle Street
Dalkey
County Dublin
285 0552

Asheesh Dewan's George's Street flagship has been hailed in various quarters as the best Indian restaurant in the city, and the Dalkey branch continues his quest for culinary enlightenment. The grotty Al Minar Tandoori has been totally refurbished, and elegant furniture, fine tableware and courteous service now make this a soothing oasis in the heart of the village. Chef Amit Wadhawan – whose influences are more coastal than southern – has an equally delicate touch, so you won't leave needing a twelve hour nap. Must-haves include Mahi Kalimiri, stir-fried tiger prawns, chickpea pancakes and exotic fruit chutney (€10.80) and the Murgh Tak-a-Tin, chargrilled chicken and caramelised yellow and red peppers in a tangy tomato sauce (€15.90). Traditional extras like poppadums and naans get the gourmet treatment and the menu is available for take-away at a 20% discount.

Indian CD

"Who drinks our wines?"

Andrea Roche
*Former Miss Ireland and Dublin's
very own "It Girl"*

Brian McGinn,
*Woodford Bourne Profiles in
Excellence Award winner,
Young Designer of the Year 2002*

"We do"

For Andrea and Brian wine is a way of life. From the
very first 'pop' of the cork from a bottle of Freixenet's
sexy Spanish cava, to the last sip of the final glass in one
of Ireland's coolest clubs. Get that 'hip' feeling by trying
the exclusive range of Freixenet sparkling wines from
Woodford Bourne

"what's your story"

A commitment to excellence for 250 years

A Member of the DCC PLC Group

Kilkenny Design Centre

6 Nassau Street
Dublin 2
677 7066

If you're meeting mummy for a cup of cocoa, or dumping
your lousy lover, don't forget the large, mezzanine café in the
very cool Kilkenny Design Centre. It's the perfect place for a
cosy chat or a large, public spat. Why? The food and service
are old-fashioned, homely, but the interior is bright,
dramatic. Yes, that's not quite logical, but then, why would
anyone want to eat in a shop? Well, there's the seafood
chowder (€4.45) for instance – as good a brew as you'll find in
many fancy restaurants. Follow it with the Tuscany panini
(tuna fish, tomato and basil, €6.30) or, for real comfort
eating, the peanut butter baguette (€3.10). There are lots of
gluten-free dishes on the menu – including cakes and soups.
And if you're really too busy to get out, phone your sandwich
order in and have it delivered to the office.

The King Sitric

East Pier
Howth
County Dublin
(*832 5235*

Something of a Dublin classic, but don't let that put you off:
Joan and Aidan MacManus have now renovated their
restaurant and rooms overlooking Howth harbour. These
days you'll be welcomed in the new bar area, shown to your
table, offered drinks and issued with a cheerful invitation to
poke around the temperature controlled wine cellar; it is
indeed impressive, with a vast selection of classic French
wines. For starters try the buttermilk crab bake (€12.70), or
the grilled scallops with black and white pudding (€10.80).
Stick to seafood mains, like pan-fried lemon sole or the
seafood medley – mussels, oyster, crab, prawns and squid in a
white wine sauce. Both feature on the €45 four course dinner
menu. Service was disorganised the last time we ate here, but
that may be unusual; readers of *The Dubliner* rave about this
classy northsider.

 Seafood

Kish

Coliemore Road
Dalkey
County Dublin
285 0377

Bono and Neil Jordan are regulars at this expensive fish restaurant, which was widely tipped as a Michelin contender when it opened in 2000. Kish has an enviable location and arguably the best view of any restaurant on the east coast. The tables are well spaced, the lighting is intimate, the glassware is tasteful and there is an air of luxury throughout. Today, however, the service is sniffy and the food is merely adequate. Last time we ate here, there were just two meat main courses available. Neither venison nor guinea fowl have universal appeal, so the fish would need to be very good indeed. Brill, John Dory, salmon and cod were all presented in exactly the same fashion – a small portion of fish delicately balanced on a little mound of vegetables or mashed potato. No real flair, and in most cases the fish was overcooked. A shame, as the venue is fantastic.

Formal CD

Lemon

66 South William Street
Dublin 2
672 9044

By all means, forget the weary hype about South William
Street being the most fashionable address in town – but don't
overlook this little gem. If you ever wonder why some
restaurants take off and some merely slumber, take a look at
Lemon. Like all the best concepts, it sounds simple – crepes,
sandwiches, coffee. This tiny pancake joint is distinguished
by great style, good, cheap food (the most expensive crepe is
the smoked delux, €4) and charming service, personified by
owner Adrian Reynolds (pictured right). Our only quibble is
that Lemon should be open later, for perfect post-pub grub.

PUNDIT PIE | *My favourite Italian is Da Roberto in Blackrock.
Ross Lewis is an inventive chef at Chapter One. The most irritating
thing about dining in Dublin is bad service. Have we come a long
way in terms of quality? Yes. Do we get value? Rarely. In terms of
trends, I think there will be a lot more fusion cooking in the next few
years – **Paolo Tullio** is the Irish Independent restaurant critic.*

2 Cheap and Cheerful

The Lobster Pot

9 Ballsbridge Terrace
Dublin 4
660 9170

Tom Crean's old-school fish restaurant makes few concessions to the fickle whims of fashion. Dedicated regulars clearly enjoy the fact that Christmas fairy lights hang in the windows all year round. The gentle, old-fashioned courtesy of the all-male staff is refreshing, and their strict adherence to traditional Silver Service is utterly charming. The day's catch is wheeled to your table on a trolley and every possible cooking method is discussed at length. Many dishes come with rich, creamy sauces, but staff are equally happy to grill your choice and serve it plain. Don't leave without trying the prawn bisque, probably the best in Dublin.

PUNDIT PIE *Are there 100 good restaurants in Dublin? Unlikely. Where do I go to eat for pleasure? The dumplings at China Sichuan are the best in the country. I also like the Empress Garden in Monkstown. You can't beat Guilbaud's lunch. And L'Ecrivain is still one of my favourites. Ely has good food and an unbeatable wine list. I also like the Mermaid. Most over-rated »*

Locks

1 Windsor Terrace
Portobello
Dublin 8
454 3391

Don't come to Gavin O'Reilly's favourite restaurant to moan about the prices. With wonderful ambience, a classic interior and one of the best waiting teams in town, Locks is one of those quintessential Dublin experiences. That's why it continues to enjoy huge support and a superb reputation. The French/Irish cooking is solid rather than spectacular, although we were pleasantly surprised on our last visit. Incidentally, spuds are something of a speciality: a starter of potato skins with prawns, spinach, hollandaise and smoked salmon (€14.65) are dreamy, and the Monte Carlo potatoes (€2.70) are a perfect side order.

> *restaurant? There are so many! Mao? La Stampa? In general, there is too much too much cheffy food in Dublin, too many wine lists written by wine merchants, too little emphasis on excellence of raw materials, mind numbing predictability, crap service and, in most places, a passion by-pass –* **Tom Doorley** *is the Sunday Tribune Restaurant Critic.*

Formal 8

The Lord Edward

23 Christchurch Place
Dublin 8
454 2420

According to the *Lonely Planet Guide to Dublin*, "you'd have to be trying pretty hard not to eat well in Ireland's capital." This delightful nonsense comes from the same genius who says "no one need fear overcooked vegetables and shrivelled fish." The truth (as real Dubs know) is that it's very hard to find good seafood restaurants in the city. That's why Burdocks is so popular. A distant relative (richer/more expensive) the Lord Edward lives two doors down, three flights above a pub of the same name. Try the prawns Neuberg (€22.20) or the fat Yank's favourite: sole Lord Edward (€22.20) served in a creamy white wine and lobster sauce and stuffed with smoked salmon. Neither of these dishes are particularly modern or especially memorable – but they do keep tourists happy.

Mao

The Pavilion
Dun Laoghaire
County Dublin
214 8090

Mao is pleasant, easy, customer friendly – nothing, in short, like the brutal dictator (can you imagine a restaurant called Hitler?). The Asian (con)fusion cuisine offers good value, even if it's rarely spectacular. Stick to staples like chilli squid, Thai fishcakes, Nasi Goreng, or the lemongrass and chilli tiger prawns. Table turnover is high, and the staff all seem to like working here, so it usually has a vibrant atmosphere. On a sunny day, grab a table outside, swig a bottle of Tiger beer and pretend that Dublin has *always* been so chilled. With branches in town and Scotland, this cheerful chain looks set to expand even further next year.

La Maison des Gourmets

15 Castle Market
Dublin 2
672 7258

This bright, clean, first floor salon is midway between Brown Thomas and Costume, and portions wouldn't interfere with the strictest of diets – perfect for social X-rays. Sounds as if we're damning with faint praise, but the food is so good it doesn't matter that there's so little of it. Try the rocket and parmesan salad (€8.50), a heap of fresh, tasty leaves with exactly the right amount of parmesan or the aubergine tartine (€7.50). Follow this up with really good coffee, then stock up on bread, croissants and delicious *tarte aux poires*, all baked on the premises. Incidentally, they've just started selling their breads to Dunnes Stores – hopefully that won't affect the quality here. Finally, don't leave without prising some juicy gossip from Penny, who used to do all the private catering gigs for Patrick Guilbaud.

French 2

The Mermaid

69/70 Dame Street
Dublin 2
670 8236

Despite its utilitarian seating, there's something almost bookish about this new-Dublin classic. The *Irish Times* often have their Christmas party here and local literati linger over Chardonnay well into the afternoon (John Banville loves Saturday lunch). Owners Mark Harrell and Ben Gorman say that when it opened, there was an American bent to the Mermaid cuisine; they now prefer the term mid-Atlantic. Either way, they do a mean rib eye steak, fine salads and a great brunch at the weekends. We love the New England crabcakes (€7.75) and the pecan pie (€6.30) and we're not alone: foodies *rave* about the Mermaid. The wine list is excellent (they personally import wines from small producers on the continent). Service has always been superb too: manager Ronan Ryan is a capable guy, and most of the staff are gorgeous, which never hurts.

La Mère Zou

22 St. Stephens Green
Dublin 2
661 6669

Eric Tydgadt's basement-level bistro is cosy and romantic; perfect for those evenings when you're longing for a little bit of France. But Eric is Belgian, which the very clued-in might gather from the menu – traditional bistro fare like Moules Marinière, Steak Frites, Goat's Cheese Salad and that stout Belgian favourite, Waterzoe. Although the food is not quite as authentic as you'd find in some dirty little café in Bruxelles, it is usually good and plentiful. The staff, most of whom are French, are pleasant, and the warm ambience appeals to a loyal clientele.

PUNDIT PIE *Kevin Thornton is our best chef, but not necessarily my favourite. The Commons is the most over-rated restaurant in the city. I felt rushed when I was there last, and was surprised to note spelling mistakes on the menu. The Unicorn has the best atmosphere of any restaurant here –* **Georgina Campbell** *edits the Jameson Guide.*

French 2

Moe's

112 Lower Baggot Street
Dublin 2
676 7610

Moe's occupies one of the most famous restaurant spaces in
the country. On the one hand, Conrad Gallagher had his very
first restaurant here. On the other hand, so did Derry Clarke.
A drama about their contrasting fortunes would look well on
television, but not the silver screen: Moe's is tiny. Still, who
says big is better? Elaine Murphy is a passionate restaurateur
and her staff seem enthused rather than merely employed.
Ad-world honchos and media types rub shoulders (literally)
while tucking into modern Irish classics like the confit duck
leg (€20.95) stuffed with rhubarb and ginger, served with
sweet potato cake, spiced cabbage and chilli jam.

Montague Brasserie

4B Montague Street
Dublin 2
478 1535

For many years the Montague was Dublin's most notorious greasy spoon: dodgy gamblers rubbed shoulders with young cops, all night revellers and local suits in a scene from a Robert Altman movie. Today, a late night restaurant has taken its place. Run by Carsten Juchatz and Joan Daly – you may remember her as the singing manager of George's Bistro – this tiny restaurant is open until 2.30am. Eclectic menu: pizzas and pasta, a chargrilled 10oz sirloin steak with garlic butter, and more ambitious fare, like a braised lamb shank with garlic and rosemary (€15.00). Try the steamed mussels with shallots, garlic and white wine cream. At €6.25 it's almost a meal in itself, and a vast improvement on chipper fare – which, let's face it, is what you usually find at two in the morning. Incidentally, keep an eye out for neighbour Noelle Campbell Sharpe, regaling her army of bright young things with tales of derring-do – and lessons in life well lived.

Nosh

111 Coliemore Road
Dalkey
County Dublin
284 0666

Frankly, we'd like to keep Nosh to ourselves, but that would be selfish. It's a tiny place, really, no more than 40 seats, but Nosh has great atmosphere (particularly at night), excellent lighting, stylish, modern interiors – think Bang crossed with Expresso Bar – and jolly good food. Indeed, it's what many casual restaurants try (and dismally fail) to be. Two bright sisters, Samantha and Sacha Farrell, both trained under the inimitable Ann Marie Nohl. Today they have a couple of strong chefs – Paul Quinn (ex-Hungry Monk) and Dave Gallagher (ex-Caviston's) – chained to the range. Fine modern Irish cuisine, and particularly good seafood: Neil Jordan loves the prawn pil-pils (€7.95) with garlic and chillies. If that doesn't appeal, try the crab claws (€7.95) and follow them with the deep fried fish and chips (€16.50).

Nude

Suffolk Street
Dublin 2
(676 1367

Siblings are a nightmare at the best of times, but spare a
thought for Norman Hewson. Kid brother Paul is a big-shot
rock star – and as if that's not enough, the little brat is also
trying to save the world! So what can you do? Open a
restaurant. But not just any old restaurant. Nude is a
'concept' restaurant. And the concept is sound: super-fresh
food, prepared on the premises, served by angels and sold for
next to nothing. Sounds simple, but Norman is not one to
rest on his laurels: the menu is constantly changing, and the
concept just gets better. Our current order? A large bowl of
seafood chowder (€5), a pastrami panini (€4.50) and a large
banana smoothie (€3.75). Incidentally, Nude is also one of
the most popular pick-up joints in the city. Take a seat on the
benches; eat, meet and toast the mighty Hewsons.

Number Ten

Longfields Hotel
10 Lower Fitzwillian Street
Dublin 2
676 1367

Longfield's – a boutique hotel – boasts a basement restaurant, in which Kevin Arundel is quietly carving a reputation for very fresh, very tasty fare. Arundel's cooking holds its own in an area that is fast becoming Dublin's culinary quarter – indeed, there are plans afoot to formalise this. Number 10 has a soft Georgian feel and, although it's small, diners are afforded plenty of room for intimate chit-chat – it's a useful refuge for stressed execs and middle-aged lovers. The table d'hote dinner (€40) offers good value and a wide selection, which includes seared fillet of John Dory with crushed new potatoes and a Nicoise salad, or pot-roast rabbit with foie gras and a saffron risotto. Mr Arundel is a talented chef – and this little restaurant is well worth discovering.

Modern European 2

Ocean

Charlotte Quay Dock
Dublin 2
668 8862

Ocean must have the best summertime location in the city –
not to mention easy access if you're sailing in from out of town.
And following a *very* rocky start, it is finally settling down.
Aging models and young copywriters love the "space, man,"
which makes great use of views and natural light. After
abandoning the attempt to be a fine dining restaurant, much
of the menu is now glorified bar food: seafood chowder
(€6.25), oysters (€7.80), a selection of pastas (average €12.50)
and fancy salads (average €11). Nut and gluten free dishes are
indicated as such – bravo! On our last visit, the marinated lamb
with potato rosti (€16) and cod with wilted greens (€12.50)
were both unremarkable – and portions are small.

Odessa

13 Dame Court
Dublin 2
670 7634

You've got to hand it to them: in less than a decade, Jay
Bourke and Eoin Foyle single-handedly re-invented nightlife
for Dublin youngsters. Their collection now includes Ri-Ra,
Gubu, The Globe and Eden – amazingly, all are still cool
places to see and be seen in, years after opening. This flagship
lounge-cum-restaurant has never pretended to offer *haute
cuisine*, but the food – try the quesadillas (€11.50) or the
organic beef burger with smoked bacon and homecut chips
(€11.25) – is always comforting, prices are modest and the
mojitos are top-notch. If you're feeling particularly dark and
moody, make sure you sit downstairs. Plus: best looking staff
in the city, ably led by young Dave Spencer. Finally, brunch on
Sunday is particularly popular with weekend hippies.

One Pico

Molesworth Place
Schoolhouse Lane
Dublin 2
676 0300

It is unfair to compare the current One Pico to its former home on Camden Street– but absolutely necessary, as this is the only way to understand the great strides Eamon O'Reilly has made since first becoming a chef/proprietor. In the handsome premises once occupied by the glamorous Polo One – where socialites and errant secretaries had long, boozy lunches – you will find decent grub at reasonable prices. Food is mature, confident. Try the tempura of smoked haddock with sweet potato and lime pickle (€11.36), which looks very dreary but tastes divine: think fancy Indian fish with spicy-sweet chips – good flavours and not too heavy. Fillet of veal (braised in chicken stock), served with sautéed ceps mash, baby spinach and truffle cream is truly excellent (€24.76), as is the fillet of beef (€24.06). Waiting staff are friendly and efficient. Finally, One Pico is a good spot for first dates and anniversaries; all very romantic.

Formal 2

The Old Schoolhouse

*Coolbanagher
Church Road
Swords
840 2846*

There are few good restaurants on the northside of the city – that observation has nothing to do with snobbery. Blame history and geography. However, if you're picking someone up from the airport or you live in the area, check out this very distinctive eaterie. Brian and Anne Sinclair have created a comfortable restaurant out of classrooms in an old school house. Head chef Paul Lewis has been with them for ten years and offers contemporary Irish cuisine with French influences. Adventurous youngsters will enjoy the roast Barbary duckling (€23.49) and the ostrich medallions (€24.76), while parents sensibly stick to fish specials (try the king prawns or the baked crab with mushrooms and onions). There's a small patio (just four tables) which is nice in the sunshine and – on the few occasions we've eaten here – service was good.

CD Modern European

The Osborne

Portmarnock Hotel and Golf Links
Portmarnock
County Dublin
846 0611

Stick to the seafood – fresh from Howth – at this fancy hotel restaurant. Named after Walter Osborne, who painted many pictures in the area, this 80-seater is part of the impressive Portmarnock Hotel and Golf links, where Michael Douglas and Catherine Zeta Jones stayed last summer. Stefan Matz prides himself on using local ingredients throughout, and although it's not cheap – starters average €12.90 – the Osborne is certainly worth discovering. Best dish? Fillet of sea bass with mussels in a saffron sauce (€24.90). Booking essential: it's only open for dinner, and closed on Sundays and Mondays.

PUNDIT PIE *Best tactic is to decide what the evening, or your hunger, is worth. Either invest in the expertise, panache and quality of Kevin Thornton or Guillaume le Brun at Restaurant Patrick Guilbaud, or enjoy comfort food and good produce at no-frills C-Bar or Gruel. Whatever, just try to avoid inflated prices and aspirations –* **Louise East** *of the Irish Times.*

Formal CD

Patrick Guilbaud

The Merrion Hotel
21 Upper Merrion Street
Dublin 2
676 4192

PGs leaves many cold – don't get stuck with the bill – but fans rave about this little piece of France in Dublin, where all the toffs scoff and *nouveaux riches* swill aging claret. If you're the sort of person who thinks wealth is more impressive than wisdom, you will certainly leave with a sore neck. Still, this Michelin two-star has the smartest dining room in the city. The service is extraordinary (or simply irritating) and Guillaume le Brun is arguably the best classical French chef in Ireland (beware of modest portions). A first class collection of modern Irish art will satiate even the most jaded palate. Besides, they've survived twenty years in business – an achievement in itself – and they're chasing a third Michelin star, which would really put Dublin on the culinary map. Bottom line? You love PGs or you hate it. Either way, you really ought to find out.

2 Formal

Pearl

20 Merrion Street Upper
Dublin 2
661 3627

Don't forget about Sebastien Masi and Kirsten Batt's little
gem. Tucked away in a basement off Merrion Street – right
next door to Restaurant Patrick Guilbaud – it is easy to
overlook Pearl. Still, a reasonable lunch menu offers old
favourites like a plate of oysters (€10) and steak with French
fries and shallots (€22). À la carte highlights include crispy
prawns with mango and black pepper dressing (€12) and
whole pound blue lobster with garlic butter (€45).You may
not like being in a basement, and the chilly modern decor is
striking rather than comforting, but good service,
meticulous attention to detail and damn good food all
merit business. Incidentally, they have now introduced live
music on Thursday nights, which normally frightens us
away, but works quite well here.

French 2

Poppadom

91a Rathgar Road
Dublin 6
490 2383

Miriam O'Callaghan and Ulick O'Connor are regulars at this suburban Indian, one of the city's best. Head chef Jagdish Parshad worked in the Eastern Tandoori and Tulsi before joining the good ship Poppadom, while manager Zerxes Ginwalla was whisked away from Saagar, via London's Café Spice Namaste, to front a slick and courteous team. Very Bombay-minimalist interiors. Good, pricey Indian fare – main courses average €18. Be warned: you won't be having a lager with that curry. Standout dishes include lamb Chettinad (€14.60), a South Indian specialty – onion and tomato based sauce, with fennel, peppercorn, coriander and garlic. Incidentally, Poppadom now has a takeaway branch in Newlands Cross.

Il Posto

10 St. Stephen's Green
Dublin 2
  679 4769

Danny Dorian is quite a player; a former jockey, the young
Italian-American has sponsored the polo, broken Irish hearts
and opened Il Posto since arriving here in 1997. Today his
Italian restaurant at the top of Grafton Street is managed by
the affable Amanda Jackson – you may remember her from
Little Caesars – and it does good business. The chefs and
waiters are all Italian, and the menu showcases an impressive
selection of antipasti, soups, fish, meat and poultry. On
Monday nights, Danny dons a tocque and cooks for off-duty
chefs, which is impressive. However, as the great Paolo Tullio
once admitted, "If I'm honest, I have to say that I can think of
plenty of simple, unpretentious trattorias in Italy where I'd
eat better." So the search continues for a really first-class
Italian restaurant in Dublin. We haven't found one yet.

Italian 2

Il Primo

16 Montague Street
Dublin 2
478 3373

New money icons like Denis O'Brien and Annrai O'Toole are
regulars, but Dieter Bergman is the main attraction at this tiny
Italian in the self-styled Village Quarter – a cynical bid to mimic
the horrors of Temple Bar. The eccentric German runs his bright
cheerful restaurant like an intimate dinner party, with much
laughter, hearty pasta, lashings of gossip and stunning wine.
None of this comes cheap (except the talk, of course) but Il Primo
is well worth discovering. The food is usually excellent: start with
the pan-fried strips of marinated sirloin (€9.90), then try the
open ravioli with chicken, Parma ham, mushroom and white
wine cream sauce (€20.10). If you're feeling particularly flush, go
for the whole roasted sea bass stuffed with fresh herbs, served
with baby roast potatoes and asparagus (€28.95). The service is
superb and Dieter is such a priceless character that you almost
feel lucky to have swelled his pockets.

2 Italian

Queen of Tarts

4 Cork Hill
Dame Street
Dublin 2
670 7499

If you haven't been into the newly refurbished City Hall (cost: €4 million) do nothing else until you rectify this. Nowhere will make you prouder of your city than this classic 18th century building. Once you've done the tour, consider lunch in Queen of Tarts – but head for the original across the road on Dame Street rather than the cramped underground café on the premises. Word of mouth is fast establishing this tiny café as one of the best places for cheap, home-cooked food. Excellent gourmet sandwiches (from €3.40), soup (€3.30), Greek salad (€6.30) and savoury tarts (from €6.90) provide the build-up to the real business of the menu – pudding. Enjoy cakes, tarts, bread-and-butter pudding and every other sweet treat you dimly remember, all in a space so cosy it could have been designed by Beatrix Potter.

QV2

14/15 St. Andrew Street
Dublin 2
677 3363

Two mixed experiences: Friday night, seven o'clock. Bright
yellow walls, a mild whiff of detergent in the air. American
tourists use a calculator to convert the price of the early bird
menu. Staff are idling, the food is mediocre. Monday lunch: one
of the two dining rooms is packed, a cheerful Australian
waitress is keen to please. The leek and potato soup (€5) is fresh,
tasty, just the thing for a cold, wet summer afternoon. Corned
beef with champ and mashed potato (€10) is splendid. John
Count McCormack is a bit of a character – long grey pony tail,
apparently plays in a band. His restaurant is no match for the
man himself, as it badly needs a little atmosphere, and has too
many tables, arranged in classroom fashion. But Eoin
McDonnell is not a bad chef, the prices aren't *too* extravagant,
and QV2 is always reliable, if never spectacular.

Ragazzi

109 Coliemore Road
Dalkey
County Dublin
284 7280

The best pizza in town or the sleaziest restaurant this side of Naples? We'll let you decide. Ragazzi means 'guys' in Italian; that perfectly describes this small, buzzy bistro in the heart of Dalkey, run by ex-Pasta Fresca manager Paolo and his trusty band of stallions. If you're feeling low and need a bit of an ego boost, these guys will certainly oblige, with corny chat-up lines and falsetto opera serenades – no wonder it's a favourite with posh Dalkey matrons. Ragazzi is also a beloved haunt of local glitterati (the stairwell is covered with rock star autographs) who clearly appreciate value. Try the bruschetta, piled high with luscious ripe tomatoes and garlic (€4.95), carpaccio with rocket and generous shavings of parmesan (€ 7.25), and wonderful pasta dishes. But pizzas steal the show, with the thinnest, crispiest bases in... Dublin?

The Red Bank

7 Church Street
Skerries
County Dublin
849 1005

With his long, unruly beard, gregarious personality and championing of Irish cooking abroad, Terry McCoy is one of the great characters of the Irish restaurant business. This handsome showcase for his contemporary (ish) Irish cuisine is perfect for those special-occasion dinners that merit the trip to farflung suburbs. McCoy uses fresh local produce throughout; his seafood dishes are particularly good. Start with the creamy seafood chowder (€3.95) and follow it with the monkfish (€16.50) or the sole and oysters "Táin Bo" on the table d'hote (€29) menu. Charlie Haughey loves the old-fashioned dessert trolley.

CD Seafood

Roly@The Pavilion

Unit 8, The Pavilion
Dun Laoghaire
County Dublin
236 0286

Roly Saul says this is Roly's for the 21st century, and he's right:
think Roly's Ballsbridge without the steak and chips expense
account crowd. Think a lighter, fresher Roly's. Everything is a
bit less fussy, less sir and madam. If the old Roly's is the Moulin
Rouge – ornate food, ornate decor and ornate service – then
Roly@The Pavilion is The Hacienda. The dining room is vaguely
modern, sparse, with chi-chi booths, a nod to the classic
American diner. A good take on the old goat's cheese to start –
piccalili instead of the more familiar and boring fruit chutney.
Or try the rare tuna with a ginger spring roll; incredibly fresh
and generous hunk of tuna. Follow it with the sea bass; simple,
nicely crisped skin, plenty of it. Don't get the wrong idea: we still
love Roly's in Ballsbridge. It's where you'd bring your folks for a
slap up dinner. But this is where you'd bring your sexy aunt.

Modern Irish **CD**

Roly's Bistro

7 Ballsbridge Terrace
Dublin 4
668 2611

One of the great characters of the Irish restaurant business, Colin O'Daly has his hands full, now that he's bought out partner Roly Saul and launched a Palm Beach branch. Thankfully, Colin hasn't left the kitchen altogether, and when he's away, *chef de cuisine* Paul Cartwright is a fine sub. Despite minor issues – your wine won't be opened at your table, upstairs is smarter than downstairs – we still love Roly's. It's wonderfully warm and inviting, the service is usually good, prices are reasonable and the restaurant is always busy, but *never* chaotic. O'Daly's cooking is solid and unfussy, based around the principles of good, hearty bistro food; there's plenty of imagination here too. Try the duck spring roll with stir-fried noodles (€8.95) and follow it with Dublin Bay Prawns with garlic, ginger and chili butter (€21.50). All in all, a Dublin classic.

3 Modern Irish

Seasons

Four Seasons Hotel
Simmonscourt Road
Ballsbridge
Dublin 4
665 4642

Opinions are still divided on the architectural merits of the Four Seasons. Frankly, this debate looks set to run and run – but then, so will the hotel itself. The staff are so well trained that even the most cranky demands are met with a smile. We love the bar – the only classic American-style bar in Ireland. Try the bramble cocktail or a chocolate martini, and soak it all up with chips and truffle aïoli. We first sampled the main restaurant on Christmas Day – hardly an ideal time to judge it. Still, we had a rip-roaring time – worth bearing in mind if you couldn't be bothered to stuff that turkey. We went back for more last month, and came away laughing again – John Healy is the most entertaining maitre d' in town. Try the fillet of beef with truffled mashed potato, caramelised vegetables and a pinot noir sauce. At €45, the set dinner menu offers good value for a restaurant of this calibre, and Sunday brunch is already a D4 staple.

4 Formal

Shanahan's on the Green

119 St Stephen's Green
Dublin 2
407 0939

There are many reasons to rave about John Shanahan's upscale American restaurant. Under manager Martin Clegg, the service is impeccable – fancy, not too formal – and the interior oozes money. We love the clubby bar downstairs, where bartender Kevin Hennessy keeps the wisecracks flowing as quickly as the bourbon, star-spangled studs hold court with young admirers, and the Corrs (still) try to crack that US market. The menu has a light sprinkling of Irish favourites (like Galway oysters) and sublime desserts. New Yorkers write home about the classic American sides, like creamed sweetcorn and onion rings. But the real treat here is the prime fillet of beef, sourced from Shanahan's farm in County Meath. It's not cheap, and the portions are designed for body-builders, but you won't find a better steak anywhere in Ireland today.

Formal 2

The Shelbourne

27 St Stephen's Green
Dublin 2
663 4500

During the Easter Rising, rebels stopped sniping from the roof of the Royal College of Surgeons every morning, to allow the Shelbourne doorman to feed the ducks in St Stephen's Green. Traditions are still preserved at the grand old dame of Dublin hotels (last year Bono queued up like everyone else to get in on Christmas Eve) even though the Shelbourne is owned by Scots and Japanese bankers and managed by a Frenchman, Jean Ricoux. There are many sides to this old-school classic: like the Horseshoe Bar, where married men mingle minus rings. There's the Side Door (decent bistro food) and Number 27, a very grand dining room, where you'll find the best breakfast in the city (€22), and a fine roast for lunch. But our favourite part of the Shelbourne is the Lord Mayor's Lounge. Civilised, elegant, and blissfully soporific, it's a dreamy refuge from a city that seems more frantic than ever.

Soup Dragon

168 Capel Street
Dublin 1
872 3277

We were shooting a cover on the roof of a fancy new apartment block. The sky did all that Irish stuff – billowing high, swooping low, a riot of colour in shades of grey. Escaping from the rain, we descended *en masse* to this tiny soup kichen, across the road from Gerald Davis' gallery on Capel Street. What blessed relief. Open just a year, it already feels like a Dublin institution – why didn't anyone think of doing it like this before? The soup is fab: try the broccoli and blue cheese, the smoked haddock and potato chowder or the dahl and down it with a strawberry smoothie, great bread and free fruit. Nice touches, too, like lavish sprigs of mint in jugs of tap water. By the way, if the sun does emerge before Halloween, and you want to get all continental, try the gazpacho Andaluz. It's the best we've had in Dublin.

The Steps of Rome

Chatham Street
Dublin 2
670 5630

This unique little place, just off Grafton street, boasts cheap slices of pizza, reasonable pasta and delicious coffee. Lots of Mama Mia atmosphere, bella donna waitresses and bo-bo (bourgeois bohemian) customers. Perfect if you are on your own (partially because it is so small) and want to people watch, as being ogled from a very close distance seems part of the deal; or just relax and soak up the friendly commotion. By the way, many people rave about the pizza slices – we're not sure why.

PUNDIT PIE *Are there 100 good restaurants in Dublin? Hardly. My favourite chef is Kevin Thornton, who is well worth the prices he charges. Wagamama is the best value restaurant in the city. Guilbaud's is the most over-rated — the prices make the blood drain from my face. I would advise eating a hearty meal before and after visiting. A lot of the lavatories in Dublin restaurants are grotty. We're about to see a return to simple but wholesome foods. We'll also be seeing less fish on the menu —* **Helen Lucy Burke** *is the most feared restaurant critic in Irish history.*

The Still Room

Old Jameson Distillery
Bow Street
Dublin 7
807 2355

Don't be put off by Smithfield's burgeoning reputation as
the capital of shabby chic Dublin – and yes, we know it's still
more shabby than chic. This inviting café in the old Jameson
distillery is surprisingly good. Classic Irish comfort-food like
bacon with parsley sauce, served with cabbage and new
potatoes (€7.25-€10), or roast rib of beef with wholegrain
mustard seed (€7.25-€10), and tea time staples are offered at
reasonable prices in an area that badly needs more decent
eateries. Spot jolly Americans (sparkling, not still) and
tribunal-rich barristers out for short, boozy lunches. Have a
shot and scale the adjoining chimney at Chief O'Neill's hotel,
which offers an astonishing view of the city.

7 Traditional Irish

The Tea Room

The Clarence
6-8 Wellington Quay
Dublin 2
407 0813

The Tea Room was one of the great success stories of the Dublin restaurant world in the 1990s. Despite the usual begrudgery ("what do rock stars know about cooking?"), no parking and a criminal waste of space (why would anyone split this gorgeous room in two?) chef Michael Martin won wide acclaim. Martin moved on, but his replacement, Antony Ely – who was previously at the Square in London – is no slouch, and the Tea Room is still more hit than miss. Ely's eclectic new Irish cuisine appeals to legal and media bigshots and, of course, the pop star fraternity (yes, that *is* Elvis Costello). Best dish? Ballotine of salmon (€27) served with scallop and shrimp lasagne, asparagus and shellfish bisque. Order a side dish of truffle creamed potatoes (€7) and marvel at what can be achieved with a humble spud. At the time of going to press, an interior makeover is in the pipeline.

Thornton's

1 Portobello Road
Dublin 8
454 9067

First, the bad news: Thornton's is well located if you live in Harold's Cross. And it's *very* expensive. But Kevin and Muriel Thornton are the most ambitious couple in the Irish restaurant business. Their diligence – and Kevin's cooking – has been rewarded by a second Michelin star. This proves that the tyre-ants are catching up with common sense, but it won't change things down Portobello way. As usual, the service – under Olivier Meisonnave – will be sublime, Kevin will use too many truffles, and Muriel will scold him. Meanwhile, their many fans will continue to enjoy this suburban gem. Postscript: at the time of going to press, Kevin and Muriel Thornton were negotiating with the Fitzwilliam Hotel, with a view to taking over the space once occupied by Peacock Alley.

8 Formal

Tiger Becs

35 Dawson Street
Dublin 2
671 7113

We avoided this large dungeon for months, on the basis that
the food at La Stampa, its big brother, is usually awful – and
the room could hardly match that splendid venue. But Tiger
Becs is lots of fun, the perfect spot for late dinner with a gang
of boozy friends. Chef Charlie Phuakchoo used to work at
Diep Le Shaker; he still imports delights like lemongrass, chill
and tamarind from Thailand, and the menu reflects that
missionary zeal. Start with the Tiger's Tale (€16.50) or the
crispy fried cashew nuts (€5.50). Follow it with one of the stir
fried dishes, like monkfish with yellow sauce and spring
onions, or Kaeng Masamon (€13.50) a sweet lamb curry. Staff
are friendly, there's a great buzz about the place, and last
orders are at midnight. A pleasant surprise.

Tribeca

65 Ranelagh
Dublin 6
497 4174

Trevor Browne learned the ropes at the Elephant and Castle.
Browne pinched their recipe for chicken wings, and the name
suggests New York, but don't get the wrong idea: Tribeca
owes no favours to anyone. The large, kid-friendly menu, a
chic interior and helpful service appeal to well-heeled locals
like John Rocha and Louis Walsh (who has no kids, of
course). But let's be honest: that menu is way too big, always
a bad sign. Avoid the noodles. Try the Thai deep-fried fish
cakes with a sweet chilli and cucumber dipping sauce
(€6.33), and follow it with roast fillet of salmon with red
curry cream, spinach and jasmine rice stir-fry (€17.83). Or
try the best steak sandwich in town (€13.99). For once, the
hype proves well founded: this utilitarian diner is a welcome
addition to an urban village that badly needed a decent
neighbourhood restaurant.

The Trocadero

St Andrew's Street
Dublin 2
677 5545

Despite a recent makeover, the Troc still has an eighties buzz.
Those Tony Bennett tunes and the actors' headshots which
line the walls of this showbiz favourite lend it a timeless
twang. Maitre d' Robert Doggett runs the show with good
humour and great courtesy. Head chef Joseph Murray churns
out comfort food – big racks of lamb (€23.49), a reliable fillet
steak (€21.52) – for bitchy actors ("I slept with that prick")
who know little about life off-stage. Ignore them with all the
haughtiness you can muster. Loudly drop names like
'Pearson' and 'Stembridge.' One of the few restaurants in this
city in which you are guaranteed a memorable evening – even
if the food is erratic, to put it mildly.

2 Traditional Irish

The Unicorn

12b Merrion Court
Dublin 2
662 4757

Last time we wrote about The Unicorn, we noted that owners Jeff and Giorgio are so laid-back that surnames do not suit them. Nothing's changed on that front. The prices haven't come down either, but the Irish-Italian cuisine has improved, and we've finally found something we like: the antipasti buffet. Mind you, the food still takes second place to the atmosphere here in Dublin's most fun and stylish restaurant. For incredible service (Giorgio and his wife Noreen deserve the freedom of the city), terrific ambience, sunlit lunches on the terrace, and titillating glimpses of the city's elite – adulterous winks, dirty deals – there is nowhere like it. Except, of course, the Horseshoe Bar, where regulars go for post-prandial piss-ups. Incidentally, the entire block has been colonised by the Unicorn clan; they now have a sandwich bar, food shop and – through Chris and Simon Stokes of Bang – *another* restaurant round the corner.

Italian 2

The Vaults

Harbourmaster Place
IFSC
Dublin 1
(605 4700

Brand new, not bad: a vast space under Connolly Station has been stylishly converted into a multi-purpose venue with a restaurant and three bars. The original vaulted ceilings and exposed brick walls are handsome. They're dressed with kitsch emblems (like large stone knights, standing guard at doorways) and some chic design features. Ten vaults lead one into another, all with plasma screens and surround sound. Some have formal tables and chairs, others have great big leather armchairs. You can have lunch, dinner – until 8pm – o bar-food; Michael Martin, who used to run the Tea Room at the Clarence, oversees the kitchen. Down to earth with a bang then? Not really. The Caesar salad, chicken wings and pizzas are all good; standout dish is a damn fine steak with potato wedges and sumptuous Bearnaise sauce (€17). Promising.

Vermillion

96 Terenure Road
Terenure
Dublin 6
 499 1300

Nisheeth Tak started at Saagar on Harcourt Street, then
managed Poppadom in Rathgar, before moving to the
superb Jaipur on South Great George's Street. Vermillion,
his first venture as a proprietor, is a delight. Ignore the
location – all too typical (above a pub in Terenure). Inside?
Comfortable, spacious, stylish. The menu is Indian fusion –
lots of classics, alongside off-beat treats like duck rolls and
Goan Vindaloo – using fresh ingredients and prepared with
real passion. Presentation is a happy mix of traditional and
contemporary: crisp white tablecloths and napkins,
sparkling silver and glassware. The service is excellent, and
prices are cheaper than you might imagine – always a good
thing. All in all, the best ethnic restaurant in Dublin today.

Ar Vicoletto

5 Crow Street
Temple Bar
Dublin 2
670 8662

There's a waitress in Ar Vicoletto called Martina, who has the gift of making you feel that tonight, at least, you're the only person in the world who really matters. And the customers are equally colourful: the last time we ate here, Gavin Friday and Guggi were planning world domination on a napkin. But enough of this frippery: the food is also worth checking out. Start with the bresaola (€11.36) and follow it with rigatone con melanzone (€11.36) or the spaghetti al frutti di mare (€13.90). It's a small place, and you'll probably end up sitting on top of your neighbours, but at least there is plenty of atmosphere – unlike many (so-called) restaurants in Temple Bar. Hats off, then, to owner Luigi Santoro, the man who gave us the Steps of Rome and Ciao Bella Roma.

Wagamama

South King Street
Dublin 2
478 2152

This cheap, group-friendly Japanese noodle bar is part of a chain, and let's face it, nobody ever got engaged down here. The large basement interior is what can only be described as Pawsonesque – think long, uncomfortable benches, simple settings and lots of nude wood. You'll share those benches with savvy students, weary shoppers and office girls. Waiters take your order by scrawling on your paper place setting, which can upset the delicate diner. Start with the deep fried prawns –ebi katsu (€7.55) – and follow them with cha han (€8.85) or seafood ramen (€11.40). Wash it all down with raw juice, and pretend you're free of toxins. But don't go reaching for a fag – there's a strict no-smoking policy.

Yamamori

71 South Great George's Street
Dublin 2
475 5001

Loud and fun, this trendy Japanese offers all the usual sushi and sashimi fare at reasonable prices. It's a good starting place for norimake and tempura first-timers. Staff are very much cooler than you or I will ever be, which some folk may not appreciate. Also, Yamamori is often filled with large, noisy groups, so couples may find it less than intimate. On the plus side, portions are big. Best dish? Chilli beef ramen (€14.50). Beware: the bill mounts up rather more when you order a couple of side-dishes, but they're half the fun. Gyoza (€6.50) and deep-fried king prawns (€7.50) disappear particularly fast. Desserts don't seem especially Japanese – lemon meringue pie, chocolate cake (€6.25) – but several gallons of hot sake will produce that authentic vibe you're looking for.

Geographic Index

Category Index

Category Index

That was some meal."
          "I know, and *I* paid for it."
The food was terrible, and the
rvice was ..."
          "Darling, you should be a
          restaurant critic."
For once, you're right."

The Dubliner

**If you like this book... you'll love *The Dubliner*.
Intelligent, witty and stylish, *The Dubliner* is a magazine for
men and women who want the best in life. Join them... on a
<u>no-risk free trial</u>. Subscribe today – and receive two free
issues. If you then decide to cancel your subscription, we'll
refund your money in full.**

☐ **YES,** Please send me <u>**two free issues**</u> and start my subscription to *The Dubliner* magazine. I can cancel my subscription before receiving my third issue and get a **full refund of my money.**

☐ 1 YEAR SUBSCRIPTION
€24 PLUS €9 P+P = €33

☐ PAYMENT ENCLOSED <u>OR</u>

....

CREDIT CARD NUMBER

....

CREDIT CARD EXPIRES

NAME

ADDRESS

....

....

PHONE OR EMAIL

Return this form to *The Dubliner*, FREEPOST,
23 Wicklow Street, Dublin 2. Or Fax it to 01 675 2158.

Acknowledgements

We have always argued that it's possible to summarise the virtues and flaws of any restaurant within about 75 words, and the success of the Capital Dining pages in *The Dubliner* suggests that we are not alone. We received many requests to compile those reviews, and this is the result. So thank you, firstly, to those readers who have expressed encouragement at any stage.

We are greatly indebted to the staff of *The Dubliner* magazine, in particular to the Art Director Joanne Murphy and the Editor Emily Hourican. Further thanks are due to contributors such as Helen Lucy Burke, Tara Murphy, Will Cockrell, Tara McGinn, Louise Carolan, Bridget Hourican and Brendan O'Connor, who have all reviewed restaurants for the magazine at some stage.

Pat Austin of Woodford Bourne saw the merit of this venture as soon as we told him about it. We're very grateful to him and his colleagues at Woodford Bourne for sponsoring the book.

Many of the photographs are by Joanne Murphy, who also designed this book. However, we also used several publicity photos for the 100 best restaurants; many thanks to the restaurants and photographers in question.

Thank you to Louise East, Neil Clancy and Fiona Mulcahy for proof-reading this book.

Finally, Trevor would like to thank his parents, Alicia and Peter, stern critics and staunch supporters.